Contents

Introduction

Know this
Top tips from an expert	3
What's that invertebrate?	4
Eyes, ears and fingers first	6
How to make a spy-pot	8
Making sweep nets	9
Doing the insect dash	10
How to make pooters	12
Points on pooting	14

Clever trapping plans
Teasing trees	16
Nooks and crannies	18
Jumble trap	20
Funnel fauna	22
Bubble-wrap trap	24
Thigma-trap	26
Minibeast motel	28
Pitfall trap	30
Bucket or bottle trap	32
Old fruits	34
Old bones	36
Moth punch	38
Light traps	40

The Zoo Zone
Sluggish snails	42
Scuttle for a spider	44
Entertaining earwigs	46
Wonderful wallowing worms	48
Nature reserve for invertebrates	50
Finally… other favourites	52
Who's who	55
Further reading	58
Glossary	60

Introduction

Minibeasts are everywhere

Where do you live – in a city, in a town or in the countryside? Did you know that you share your living space with thousands of very small creatures? Most of them live quietly outside in gardens, parks and hedgerows, but are frequently difficult to spot. Sometimes a few of them enter our houses. Who hasn't seen a spider in the bath, or a beetle by the back door? These small animals are known to minibeast and creepy-crawly experts as invertebrates. Other people call them bugs (but actually, bugs are a special group of insects). If you're fascinated by these miniature animals, Minibeast Magic is for you. It's a simple guide to capturing and studying many of our common, often retiring and cunningly disguised invertebrates.

So how do you hoodwink these secretive creatures into revealing themselves? Delve into Minibeast Magic and learn a few wily dodges involving tricks, treats and smart plans designed to lure these brilliant animals near enough for you to study. No special skills are required – just a questioning mind, a bit of patience and an ability to adapt throw-away items as useful kit for bug knapping. Invertebrate-fancying friends and relatives are good to have around too!

Teasing out the timid ones

Wise up, get some tips and collect your kit

Invertebrate specialists can't really get down to business until they've collected together some useful equipment and picked up a few handy, trouble-saving tips from the experts. The beginning of Minibeast Magic covers some important first essentials and also shows you how to make your own catching devices using common everyday articles. Have someone within earshot if you need extra muscle power though.

Once you've started catching invertebrates, how do you know who they are? Over the page, there's a simplified chart putting the minibeasts into their scientifically correct groups and further on (pages 55 to 57), a picture gallery to help you identify just a few of them. If you want to be a real expert, get hold of one of the recommended identification books (pages 58 to 59).

Turn the pages

Each of the cunning traps is illustrated or its title page. Look at what stuff you'll need, follow the diagrams and read the instructions carefully. The simplest traps are on the first few pages, progressing to more adventurous ones. Think about where you're going to site some of the traps – unwary people can ruin an hour's work on a neat experiment if you don't flag it up in some way. Likely customers for your tempting decoys are also predicted on each page but be prepared for lots more and make a note of them.

Our **Ingeniously Intelligent Invertebrates** shown on every catching page, give clues, ideas and suggestions of their own, but don't stop there. You're much brighter than the average bug! Over time, after a little experience in trapping invertebrates, you too will be able to forecast which animals are likely to be found in each habitat. It's a fantastic skill.

The traps you'll be setting up shouldn't harm the minibeasts and the **Top Tips** will help you to care for them. Invertebrates should be released when your studies are complete.

What next?

Keen invertebrate specialists never stop studying the small creatures that are so vital to the health of the planet. There are tons of questions about minibeasts that need answers. If you read the last chapter, **The Zoo Zone**, you can learn how to care for some of your captives and at the same time, shed light on previously unknown invertebrate behaviour. Most importantly of all, record what you find out and hang on to the records. Scientists have been doing this for years and years and it's how they know the ways in which our natural world is changing.

HAPPY HUNTING.

Top tips

from an expert entomologist

When you catch and investigate invertebrates, here are a few points to bear in mind.

Safety

- Dress appropriately with strong shoes or wellies, but don't forget your common sense hat.
- Cover cuts and scratches with waterproof plasters and have some wipes handy.
- Watch out for where dogs and cats leave their faeces (poo) and where vegetation has been sprayed.
- Always wash your hands well after being outside.

How to be a researcher

- Have your pockets bursting with pooters, a magnifying lens, small plastic tubs, notebook and pencil. Don't go anywhere without them, you never know what you might spot.
- Wherever you go on an invertebrate hunt, remember to go quietly, tread lightly and collect calmly. You'll see so much more.
- If you lift logs or stones, always return them to their original position. Catch the uncovered animals first; put the object back then release the animals close by.
- When you work outside with trap materials, clear up after you. Leave nothing behind except your footprints.
- Apart from the animals you're investigating, take nothing away from the environment, except photographs.

Care of animals

- Check pitfall and bucket traps morning and evening, other short-term traps every 12 hours.
- Some equipment needs a sealant for fixing. Always let the smell wear off for a few days.
- You are a custodian of any invertebrates you catch, so be kind. Have their temporary homes ready for them and always return them to their habitat when you've finished observing them.
- Keep cool! Not just you – many invertebrates prefer cool shade during hot summer days. Put some damp moss, leaves or tissue in the holding containers until you release them.
- Avoid cotton wool. Its fibres get tangled in the tiny claws on invertebrates' feet – just like the Velcro™ effect.
- Try not to touch invertebrates with fingers. Ours are lumpish clumsy things, so use tweezers carefully.
- Fingering delicate butterfly and moth wings damages the covering of scales. Butterfly colours and moth camouflage are at risk when scales fall off.
- It is inevitable that you will have accidental deaths. Catching and caring for invertebrates isn't easy, especially when you're just getting the hang of things. Try not to feel too guilty about unavoidable exits – after all, how many insects are killed on the car windscreen every time you go out?

What's that invertebrate?

The following chart describes the seven major groups of invertebrates you are likely to find. The further reading list (page 58) gives sources for more detailed identification.

All invertebrates with hard exoskeletons and many legs can be grouped together as the arthropods, or 'animals with jointed limbs'. Other commonly found invertebrates are referred to as 'soft-bodied' animals.

Animals with jointed legs

Woodlice

Woodlice. These occur almost everywhere. Commonest are grey flattened forms, but also includes the pill woodlouse, capable of curling into a tight ball. Very small white woodlice are found in some ant nests. All have 7 pairs of legs. Food: rotting wood, fungi, bacteria and general detritus in damp habitats.

Millipedes

Millipedes. Most are long, slim and cylindrical. 2 pairs of legs per segment. There are some flat-backed species and a common pill millipede. Pill millipedes are darker and shinier than pill woodlice and have more legs. Food: vegetable detritus in leaf litter.

Centipedes

Centipedes. Most are long, flattened animals bearing 1 pair of legs per segment. Can have between 15 and 35 pairs of legs. Colours from dark chestnut to orange/yellow. Common under logs, stones and in soil. Food: other small invertebrate animals found in the soil, in leaf litter and under rotting logs.

Insects

All adult forms have 3 pairs of legs and bodies divided into 3: head, thorax and abdomen. All possess 1 pair each of antennae and eyes and most have 2 pairs of wings. Herbivorous and carnivorous.

1) Insects whose young are larvae with legs

Moths and butterflies (caterpillars), sawflies, beetles, fleas.

Larvae without legs
Flies (maggots, leatherjackets)

2) Insects with nymph stage

Grasshoppers and crickets, bugs (which include treehoppers, froghoppers and plant-hoppers) mayflies, damselflies and dragonflies, earwigs, lice.

Arachnids

All have 4 pairs of legs, do not possess wings and never have bodies arranged in 3 parts. Most are carnivorous.

False scorpions. Very small and found in leaf litter, compost heaps or sometimes attached to flying insect legs.

Mites. Red velvet or spider mites most commonly found. Carnivorous red velvet mites can be seen running about on walls in summer. Look like minute strawberries with legs. Red spider mites make webs on plants in greenhouses. They are sap suckers.

Harvestmen. Long-legged with small undivided body. Eyes are on a periscope near the middle of the body. Common on tree trunks and walls, also leaf litter. Mostly nocturnal. Scavengers of dead and dying invertebrates.

Spiders. Body divided in 2 parts: soft, bulbous abdomen and harder cephalothorax where legs, palps and mouthparts are attached. Can have 6 to 8 eyes. Live in many different habitats, feeding on other minibeasts often caught with silk.

Animals with soft bodies

Annelids

Worms. Earthworms are the best known. They are brown or pinky-red, long and thin and live in soil and leaf litter. Pot-worms are very thin, whitish yellow and inhabit compost in huge numbers. Food: organic matter in soil, dead plant material.

Molluscs

Slugs. Slugs have soft, mucus-covered bodies and no shell. They are common under logs, stones and other objects. Some species are specific to particular habitats. Food: Detritus, fungi and living plants. A few are carnivores.

Snails. Bodies are mucus-covered, but with added protection of a shell. Food: Similar preferences to slugs.

Important

There are no really harmful invertebrates in Britain, **but** some people are more sensitive than others to stings and bites. Be careful – don't tease creatures, especially at their biting or stinging ends. When a minibeast looks daggers at you, it's protecting itself from harm or defending its retreat from intruders. Sometimes you surprise each other, so be alert to what's around you.

To find the names and approximate sizes of the animals illustrated, turn to page 55.

Eyes, ears and fingers first

Magnifying lens

Old spoon

Small hand fork

It's a lovely warm, sunny day – perfect for being outside, so hop to it and join the invertebrates. Stand very still and look around you. What's the first thing to catch your eye? A business-like bee, a beautiful butterfly or a spider seemingly suspended in mid-air? Focus your attention. Where does the bee touch down? What's the butterfly doing? Where will the spider go next?

Making an eye on a stick

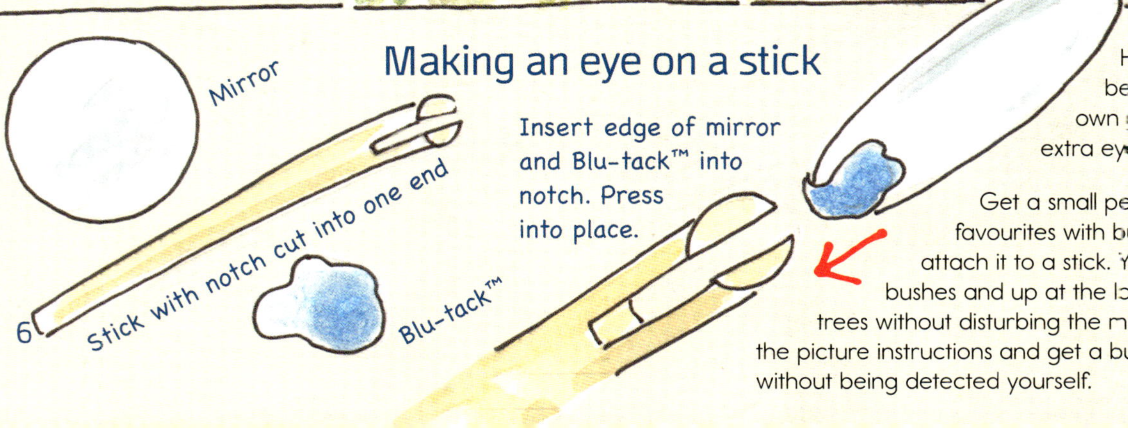

Mirror

Stick with notch cut into one end

Blu-tack™

Insert edge of mirror and Blu-tack™ into notch. Press into place.

Here's a way of beating bugs at their own game. Carry an extra eye!

Get a small pet-cage mirror, favourites with budgerigars, and attach it to a stick. You can see inside bushes and up at the lower branches of trees without disturbing the minibeasts. Follow the picture instructions and get a bug's eye view … without being detected yourself.

Squat to ground level and stare down into the 'jungle' at your feet. Concentrate on an area about the size of a large pizza and let your fingers do the walking. Push the grass and vegetation apart, search out the smallest movement, leaving no area unexplored. What do you find?

Simple tools are handy for small scale exploration too. Dig around with an old spoon or turn over a leaf pile with a hand fork.

You may not spot a minibeast immediately, but can you find where they've been? Some of them roll up vegetation to hide in, others leave silk webs behind while many more nibble greedily at flowers and leaves. Look for evidence of feeding holes and chewed out notches.

A good bug-detective keeps a sharp eye on the world. Where's that magnifying lens?

Listen too, especially on calm evenings. Can you hear any invertebrates on the move; munching, jumping, or pattering across dry leaves?

It's a hazardous world for most invertebrates. Danger is all around. Camouflage, invisibility and artful trickery are the bugs' favoured strategies for avoiding detection. You will need all your senses to notice them.

Look under bark for where beetle grubs have been. Let your fingers follow the eaten-away galleries. Are any other small creatures tucked under the bark?

Push the extra eye between leaves. Tilt the mirror to see the leaf's reflected underside. Who's there?

Look under logs and stones. Lift slowly and return gently.

How to make a spy-pot

Have you ever managed to count all the spots on a 22-spot ladybird, or check the number of legs on a centipede? This spy-pot is a simple, gentle way of restraining an invertebrate so that you can see details like patterns and other characteristics.

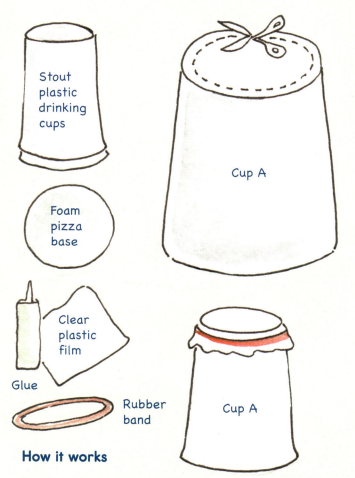

Ask an adult to cut out the centre of the base of cup A, leaving a rigid rim.

Draw round the base of cup B on the pizza base and cut out the disc. Fix the disc to the base of cup B with glue or double sided sticky tape.

While the glue is setting, stretch a piece of clear plastic film over the base of cup A and secure it with a rubber band or tape.

Put the spy-pot to one side until all the sticky parts are set. Then you're ready to examine the first specimen.

How it works

Hold cup A as if to drink from it. Put the specimen in the cup, so that it walks about on the plastic film. Push cup B down very gently and slowly towards the creature. Turn both cups upside down so that you can carefully push up the inner cup to touch your animal, but not crush it. You will see the underside details of your bug. It will be very lightly held between the soft polystyrene and the plastic film. You can adjust the tightness of hold by pulling B away from A. This gives the animal wriggle room and allows you to decide which parts you want to look at. Shake the spy-pot quickly but lightly to change the invertebrate's position. This may take a few tries. Push cup B back in place.

Now would be a good time to photograph or sketch your specimen. Release the animal as soon as you've finished looking. Plastic film can suffocate invertebrates too.

Making sweep nets

Professional entomologists, seeking insects and other invertebrates, want to capture lots of animals FAST. Their favourite bug-knapping device is a sweep net. They cut a dash through vegetation with one, and in a few minutes catch hundreds of creatures. The insects are swept off their feet and are gently buffeted into a soft and safe landing place – the bag of the net.

Here are two types of sweep net that work well. Ask an adult with strong wrists to help you.

Cheap and easy carrier bag sweep net

Open out the coat hanger to make a closed circle, but do not untwist the ends. The hook should be snipped off with pliers. Push the twisted ends into the length of cane and secure very firmly with the strong tape. Attach a robust carrier bag all the way round with staples or very strong tape.

Some animals find plastic difficult to grip onto. They might stay in the bag long enough for you to grab a pooter. In damp weather or after dew, plastic stays wet, so watch out for a puddle at the bottom of the bag.

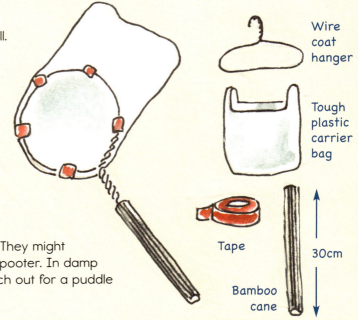

Racquet net

Remove all the strings from the racquet and fold the open edge of the pillowslip around the rim of the frame tucking it well around and underneath. Drawing pins will keep the slip on the frame if you're using Great-Grandma's wooden racquet. Ask an adult with a stapler to attach the pillowslip to a modern lightweight frame – or pull out the sewing kit and get stitching. Use the strongest thread because the net will be taking a bashing and a beating.

You can use this net nearly all year round. The pillowslip is a super-soft landing place and it's really easy to tip your catch into a sweet jar or a tray. Small creatures have feet that grip cloth well, so act fast in tipping them out.

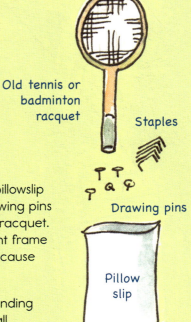

9

Doing the 'insect dash'
– using a sweep net

Keep the sweet jar containing minibeasts in cool shade. Strong sunlight and condensation can kill.

Try not to use the sweep net after rain or heavy dew. Long-legged and winged creatures are especially fragile when the sweep net bag is wet and heavy.

> Listen out for bees or wasps trapped in the sweep net. Let them out immediately.

Any time between May and early October, choose a warm sunny day and find a wide open space overflowing with flowers, grasses and even some nettles. Try to steer clear of prickly plants, although thistle flowers are favourites with many invertebrates. They also like nettles, so dust off your long trousers. Bramble and hawthorn bushes can really rip and snag sweep nets, so keep away from them.

Make sure you've got plenty of room for swishing the sweep net back and forth. Gently sweep it in a figure-of-eight movement through the vegetation, keeping the mouth of the net open all the time. Do this for several minutes so that you can catch as many unsuspecting animals as possible. Swish and sweep vegetation as often as you like, but move about so that you visit different areas. Now, gather up the top of the bag just below the frame. This is to contain the insects before you put them in a plastic sweet jar or a tray.

If you want to see how many flying insects you've caught, it's best to transfer them to a sweet jar. Sharply knock the supporting edge of the bag with your fist or against an upright object, so that the animals fall to the bottom. Lift up the bag and try to get all the minibeasts into one corner. Quickly turn the corner-full of creatures into the open top of the sweet jar by carefully pushing it inside out. Beware of crushing delicate animals. Screw the lid on as fast as you can. Inspect the catch in a shady place because strong sunlight and condensation are killers to small life. Release everything when you've finished looking. However, if some minibeasts look especially interesting, and you want to find out more, keep them for a while as 'pets'. See **The Zoo Zone** (pages 42-53) for some ideas.

Push down gently

How to make pooters

Sucking end

Bendy drinking straw

Put 'green for go' tape on suck end

Cover the end of the drinking straw with very fine mesh

Bug's entrance only

- Easy and cheap to make, so make lots at the same time.
- Give some to friends and have a pooting party!
- Catches one creature at a time, so no overcrowding.

- A lot of suck and blow makes the tubing wet and slippery. It's a good reason for having more than one.

Ask an adult for help

Every serious bug hunter needs a pooter, which works just like a mini vacuum cleaner. It collects all sorts of very small animals, but you provide the suck and then later, the blow. It is a safe and gentle way to capture invertebrates and a test of skill for you.

There are two basic designs. The first pooter is best for capturing individual animals, while the second example has a larger catching capacity, holding several animals in the same collecting jar.

Pooter One (For bug hunters who don't mind fingertips being tickled by a minibeast)

Cut the clear tubing to a 15cm length.

Cover the end of a drinking straw with mesh and hold it in position. The mesh is to stop animals from going into your mouth when you suck.

Ask an adult to dip one end of the length of plastic tubing into some very hot water to soften and expand it. Then push the meshed filter end of the drinking straw into the now pliable tubing. Wait until the wet end of the tubing has dried, then use the insulating tape to seal the joint.

Now choose a small creature to catch and have an observation container ready to put it in. Put the clear tube next to the animal and suck quickly, but calmly. It will only travel as far as the mesh on the drinking straw. Put your finger over the open end of the clear tubing to trap the creature. When you want to puff the minibeast into its own inspection pot, remove your finger and gently blow.

Pooter Two

Ask an adult to burn or drill two holes (9mm diameter) in the plastic lid of the jar. Burning holes in plastic is smelly, so is best done outside. Cut two lengths of plastic tubing, one longer than the other, or get two drinking straws. Push the tubing/straws into the holes in the lid, so that there's a tight fit. Any gaps between the tubes and the lid can be sealed with rubber solution from a puncture repair kit or with Blu-tack™.

With a rubber band, fix some fine mesh over the end of the shorter piece of tubing/straw that will be inside the pooter container. Stick some coloured tape, e.g. 'green for go' on the short 'suck' tube and/or 'red alert' on the longer 'don't suck' tube, as a quick visual reminder that small creatures will be travelling up the long tube, then down towards the container. Snap on the lid, complete with tubes, wait until the rubber solution smell has gone and prepare for pooting!

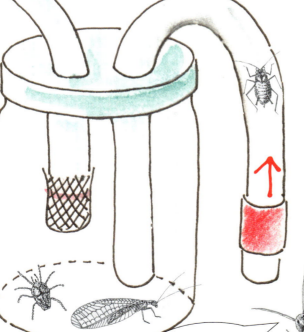

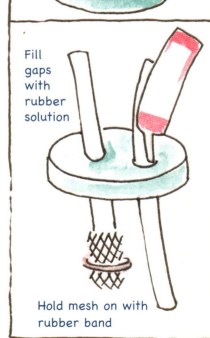

- Longer tubes give extended reaches into vegetation.
- More minibeasts can be caught in a few minutes.

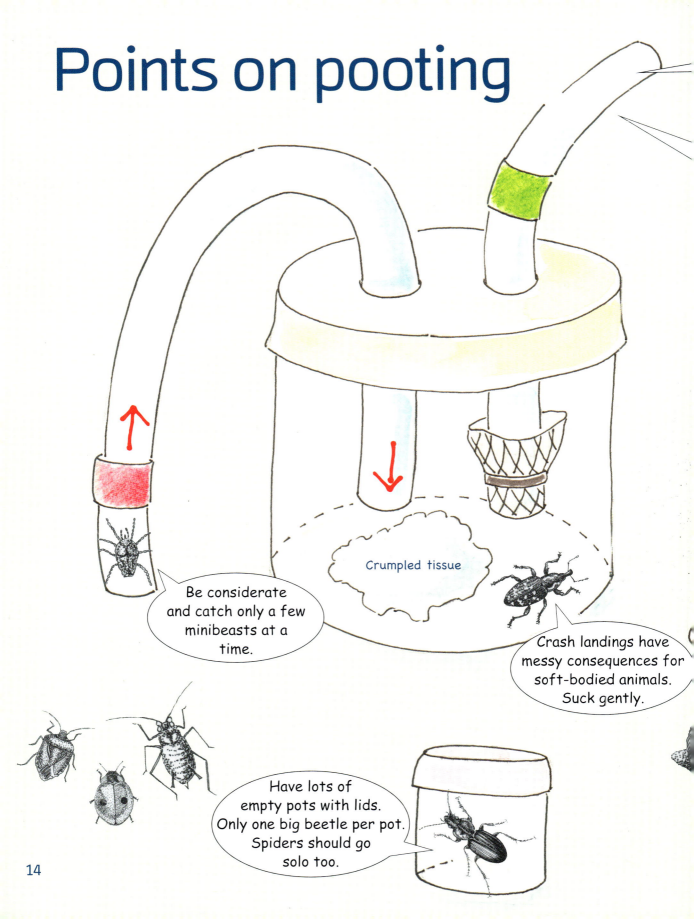

After using a pooter, sterilise the mouthpiece. Use sterilising solution for a few hours, or very hot water. Allow it to dry and it's ready for another day.

Make yours an ant-free pooter. Formic acid, exuded by some of the large ants, tastes like strong vinegar. Avoid wood ants.

Sucking up, not blasting with breath is the **Number One Rule** in pooting.

Big beetles, large woodlice, fat bugs and chunky spiders, won't go up a tight tube. Sweep them up with a paint brush and spoon, like using a dustpan and brush.

Catch animals with long legs by placing a wide-mouthed jar over them. Slide a card or similar between the mouth of the jar and the creature. Requires skill!

Slugs, snails and worms should never go in pooters – too much mucus! If you want to collect them, gently wrap in a leaf.

Teasing trees

Trees are **fantastic**. Some trees are host to hundreds of invertebrates, but to find them trees need a little teasing. Small creatures live on the trunk, on stalks, under leaves, in the flowers, and even on dead branches. Many of them show special adaptations to their particular dwelling place. Here's how to detect where they hide.

Choose a tree or bush in full leaf and open out a pale-coloured umbrella. Hang it underneath one of the branches or ask a friend to hold it. Have a stout stick ready. Give the branch a number of sharp taps but NOT a thorough thrashing. Surprised caterpillars, ladybirds, bugs and other creatures of all descriptions will fall into the umbrella ready for collection. (Don't worry – squirrels generally run up a tree!) If you don't have an umbrella, a plastic tray held under the branch or an old bed sheet spread on the ground will do.

You could also try putting the ends of very leafy branches inside a sweep net before giving some good thumps or vigorous shakes. Do this to quite a few branch ends before sampling the catch. Keep checking that the insects don't escape – they might run up the inside of the net or fly out of it.

Animals on the trunk can be more difficult to see, they are often experts in camouflage strategies. An inverted umbrella comes in useful again. Press one of the sections up against the side of the tree and with a soft brush gently dislodge any invertebrates hiding in the wider cracks and narrow fissures of the bark. Do this all round the tree, stopping every now and then to inspect the animals.

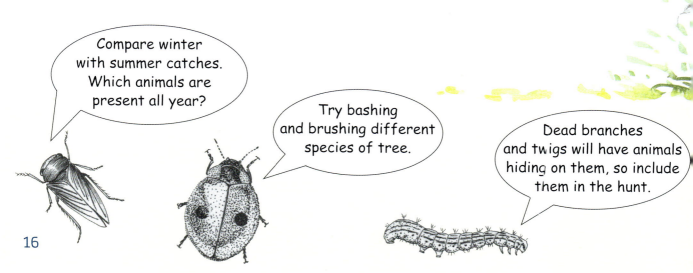

Compare winter with summer catches. Which animals are present all year?

Try bashing and brushing different species of tree.

Dead branches and twigs will have animals hiding on them, so include them in the hunt.

16

Nooks and crannies

Log piles and handmade high-rise invertebrate hotels often found on nature reserves and at wildlife centres are the ultimate in snug safety for crevice-loving bugs. However, you can make your own much simpler versions of similar habitats without trekking off to the woods. Go foraging for stuff you've got kicking around at home.

Items like cracked clay flowerpots, broken tiles, engineering bricks, piled up egg boxes, fir cones and even empty snail shells all make compact retreats for curious invertebrates. Cover them over with loosely draped and folded carpet or sacking and see who turns up to hide. Leave the trap in long grass, and away from the path of the lawnmower.

Find creatures here for your Zoo Zone pets.

Please do not disturb

What has a spider left behind?

Look for minibeast clues e.g. slime trails

Jumble trap

Does this picture look like abandoned laundry? Untidy as it seems, old items of jumble actually make first-rate shelters for invertebrates throughout the year.

Natural cotton and woollen rags can stand some of the most awful weather, but at the same time provide minibeasts with thermal protection that warms and cools slowly. Unlike plastic trap items, which collect mini puddles for animals to drown in, fabrics become wet in rain, but dry out in wind and sun, retaining some vital warmth. Choose dark and light coloured fabrics and notice the different invertebrates that are attracted.

Not everyone appreciates piles of old clothing left lying around so give plenty of warning.

Simply rumple the jumble creating plenty of creases and folds. Drape it over fences, trees or bushes but tied or pegged on firmly. Hide some under leaf piles and in compost heaps held down with netting and tent pegs. Mice and voles like warm woollies in winter, so they too might take a fancy to your cosy offerings. Un-wrap the jumble somewhere quiet so that the mammals can escape safely. This novel invertebrate hideout can be left in place for months, even until you can see green algae growing on the surfaces.

When you judge the time is right to look for any invertebrates, put the jumble trap in a plastic tray and then tease it apart.

Mice might like woollies.

Bugs love creases and trouser turn ups.

Funnel fauna

The trouble with looking for invertebrates in leaf litter is that searching them out with nothing more than fingers or tweezers can take ages. Here are a couple of less irksome and speedy ways to get them to drop out of the leaf mix. Heat, light and unpleasant odours are usually avoided by leaf-hugging minibeasts, so it's useful to take advantage of such dislikes when capturing them.

Ask an adult to cut the bottoms off three plastic plant pots. These are containers for directing light, for holding leaf litter and for captured invertebrates. Remove the top from a large lemonade bottle so that turned upside down it makes a funnel. A hacksaw blade will be useful for both operations.

Plant pot 1 stands in a tray and should have some damp tissue under it. This is the landing pad for escaping bugs. Fit the funnel into pot 1. It's the chute for delivering escaping minibeasts to the damp tissue in the tray below.

Stretch some wide mesh over the bottom of plant pot 2 and push it into the funnel. The mesh holes should allow large woodlice and beetles to fall through. Put a good few handfuls of damp leaf litter on the mesh and then push plant pot 3 on top. Here's where you can choose the method to sample the animals.

Direct an angle-poise lamp over pot 3, taking care not to melt the plastic pot. Leave for a few hours. Alternatively, place a moth repellent ball in a mesh bag resting lightly on the leaf litter. Put a plant saucer on top of pot 3 if you're using the moth ball method. It works quite quickly and minibeasts might jump all over the place.

Don't use the light and mothballs together.

Simplest of all, is to spread an old sheet on the ground, have a garden sieve ready and shake batches of leaf litter, so that animals fall through the holes onto the sheet. You might need another person to either poot up the animals or take a turn at shaking the sieve.

Plant saucer stops escapees
Plant pot 3
Plant pot 2
Moth repellent on top of leaf litter
Damp leaf litter
Mesh
Plant pot 1
Stand funnel trap on tray to contain animals
Damp tissue

Take leaves from different habitats and compare the animals. Which minibeasts live among deciduous leaves and which ones favour evergreen?

Bubble-wrap trap

Do you like popping the bubbles in plastic bubble-wrap? Well here's a good reason for not doing it! Tree-hugging invertebrates love the gaps between the bubbles, for the same reason they like the cracks in tree bark. Wrap a couple of layers round a tree or fence post and be surprised at who's tempted by a number of super-snug hideouts.

Cover with black plastic and leave for a several weeks

Follow the illustrated instructions making sure you fix everything together really well, because this trap can be left in place for a few months if you wish.

The advantage of using semi-transparent bubble-wrap is that when you remove the black bin bag, perhaps to take a sneaky preview, you can check whether any minibeasts have been tempted into hiding. Remember to replace the black covering if you want the investigation to carry on for longer.

You can also use two or three layers of corrugated cardboard instead of bubble-wrap, but it will need very robust weather proofing. Periodic peeping isn't really possible, so if you're impatient, this is a good short-term project.

When the time comes for dismantling the wraps, have a tray or sheet ready and carefully peel back the layers of plastic/cardboard into the tray.

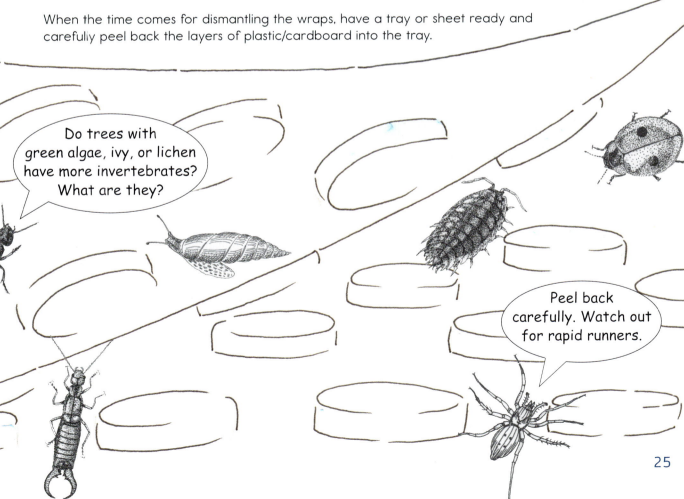

Do trees with green algae, ivy, or lichen have more invertebrates? What are they?

Peel back carefully. Watch out for rapid runners.

25

Thigma trap

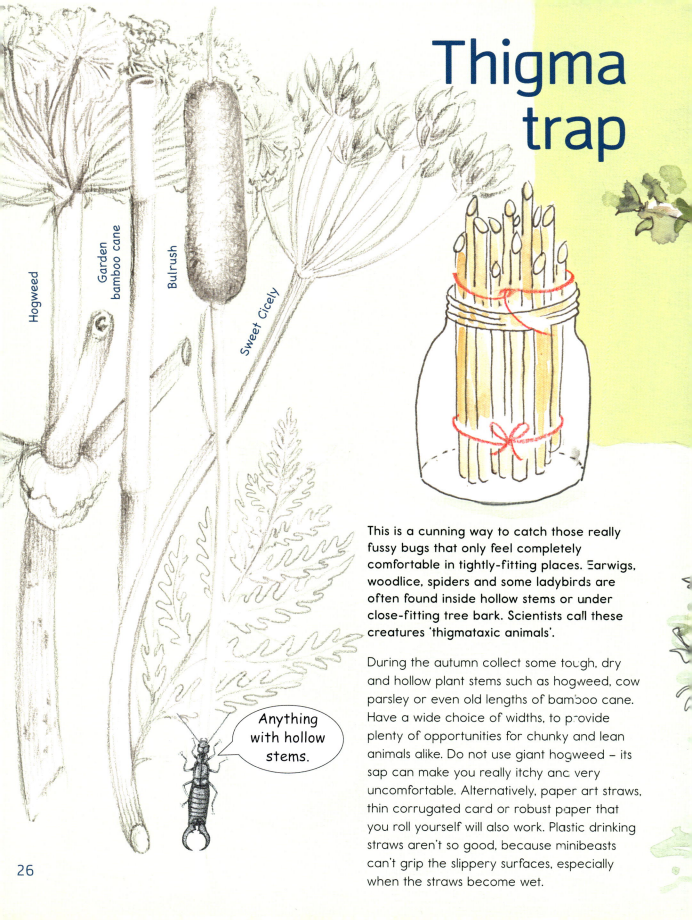

Hogweed

Garden bamboo cane

Bulrush

Sweet Cicely

Anything with hollow stems.

This is a cunning way to catch those really fussy bugs that only feel completely comfortable in tightly-fitting places. Earwigs, woodlice, spiders and some ladybirds are often found inside hollow stems or under close-fitting tree bark. Scientists call these creatures 'thigmataxic animals'.

During the autumn collect some tough, dry and hollow plant stems such as hogweed, cow parsley or even old lengths of bamboo cane. Have a wide choice of widths, to provide plenty of opportunities for chunky and lean animals alike. Do not use giant hogweed – its sap can make you really itchy and very uncomfortable. Alternatively, paper art straws, thin corrugated card or robust paper that you roll yourself will also work. Plastic drinking straws aren't so good, because minibeasts can't grip the slippery surfaces, especially when the straws become wet.

Cut the stems into lengths of about 20-30cm and tie them together securely at each end. An easy way to do this is to stand the stems in a wide-mouthed container while you tie them. Now decide on your sites, making sure the bundles are fixed very firmly and can't blow away in the next strong wind. Wait a few weeks or even some months before gently removing the bundles from the wild. Put each bundle in a plastic bag. The occupants will come tumbling out if you shake the plastic bag gently or tap each stem sharply against the inside of a plastic sweet jar or into a plastic tray. Have plenty of lidded pots ready.

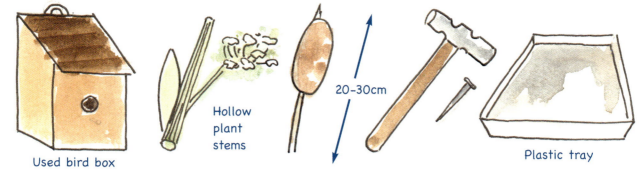

Used bird box   Hollow plant stems   20-30cm   Plastic tray

Remove front from bird box and put hanging loop on back

This is a much more robust sort of habitat offering thigmataxic minibeasts tubes, grooves and caverns held firmly in place by rigid walls and a waterproof roof. It protects long term residents and seasonal creatures from the worst of the weather, especially if you choose the site carefully.

Collect hollow plant stems or make strong paper tubes as described on the previous page. Remove the front panel from an old bird box. Fix a wire loop to the back so it will hang up. Check that the other sides and roof of the box are still substantial, and if necessary, cover them with thick polythene to keep out rain. You could also use a large plastic water carrier, but ask an adult to cut through the plastic. Another handy alternative is a large, waxed juice container. Make sure there is sufficient depth to hold lengths of stem or tubing.

Pack tightly with hollow stems

Cut the stems into lengths that will extend beyond the front of the box. Pack the stems to fit so tightly that even the stormiest weather won't dislodge them. Fill any gaps with straw or dried grass. Attach the box to a post or tree, securing it with bungee cord, rope or strong plastic twine. To hang the trap on a wall or fence use a nail or a cup hook. The trap should tilt forwards slightly to keep rain out.

Ask an adult to help attach box to tree or post

Minibeast motel

Compare what you catch in different seasons. Are there any winter residents?

After several months remove the box, unpack the stems into a tray or over a sheet and very carefully poot your catch. The kindest time to release the stem-huggers is in spring or late summer, when they'll have time to find other accommodation.

Some other invertebrates may also use the same quarters. Look for tell-tale signs such as slime trails, silk threads, sealed up stem ends and droppings.

An insect motel sited in a sunny position may attract solitary bees. Watch their comings and goings.

Pitfall trap

Try traps with or without bait.

Big game hunters used to sink pits into the ground to catch wild mammals; exactly the same method works with smaller game such as centipedes, woodlice, spiders and ground beetles.

Choose a place with short vegetation, where some animals will be running fast across dangerous wide open spaces. A little too late they will stumble across your trap, fall in … and … land close to life-sustaining lunch.

Follow the illustrated instructions to set your trap. One of the two cups, the outer one, remains sitting in the soil permanently to keep the pit in shape. The inner cup is removed each time you check the animals and change the bait. Try some slices of banana for herbivores that drop in and half a teaspoon of meaty or fishy pet food for the carnivores. Large ground beetles are voracious hunters, so a little meat prevents them from turning on any other softer-bodied captives.

The netting inserted half-way down the inner cup is to prevent unwary amphibians or small mammals from blundering into the trap. Don't let the netting touch the bait, because the animals you are trying to catch might use it as an escape ladder.

Once the trap is in position, keep out rain by covering the opening with a large flat stone or a tile. For stability balance the cover on three large pebbles, leaving plenty of gap for the animals to get underneath. **Check the trap every twelve hours.**

When you are ready to sample the invertebrates, pull out the netting, tip the contents of the inner cup into a deep-sided container and record what you find. To set the trap again, simply return the inner cup, with fresh bait, the netting and the rain cover.

Fill in the trapping hole when your discoveries are complete.

Fromage frais for one

Bucket or bottle trap

Never let last summers' well-used beach bucket feel lonely! Here's an artful new use for one as an irresistible lure for some of the higher-flying insects.

Rinse out the bucket to remove any salty sand grains. Puncture the base with a few small drainage holes and line the bottom with damp leaf litter. This layer is going to be where some insects will hide, once they've fallen into the trap. It will be cool, moist and away from the sun, but for sun-loving and mountaineering minibeasts, put a few short twigs in too.

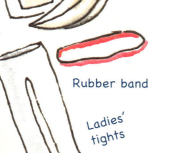
Dried yeast
Rubber band
Ladies' tights

Mash some ripe banana with a pinch of dried yeast and put the mix in the bottom of a smaller yoghurt pot, leaving a good smear of it on the rim. Cover the yoghurt pot with fine mesh e.g. tights material. By leaving the sweet-smelling bait on the rim of the pot you are bringing the aroma closer to the insects' attention and at the same time allowing them a tempting lick without the animals becoming stuck. Put this bait pot in the bucket among the leaves and then cover the bucket top with larger-mesh material. This will let the insects in, but make escape a game of chance.

WATCH OUT! Wasps are woozy in late summer.

Satsuma bag netting

Yoghurt for one
Dried yeast

Mash banana with yeast in yoghurt pot – leave tempting mix near open edge of pot

Cover with old tights and fix with rubber band
Yoghurt for one

Beach bucket

32

Suspend the bucket from a tree branch and wait for visitors. Examine the trap every twelve hours or so. Keep an eye on the bait, because the banana decomposes quite quickly.

No beach bucket? You can use a large lemonade or water bottle instead. Wash it out well, puncture the base, add leaves as hiding places and use the same bait as above – or see the Brainy Bug's ideas. If you use meaty pet food, check it frequently, especially in hot weather.

Make several of these traps and hang them in lots of different places.

Try different strong-scented baits e.g. perfumes on cotton wool or mouldy grass cuttings.

Fromage frais for one

Fishy or meaty pet food should be removed after 24 hours.

Drainage holes

Old fruits

Fruit and vegetable growers know very well that all sorts of hungry invertebrates love to snack on their crops. By leaving some of the least edible-looking fruits and vegetables outside, you can see for yourself just how many bugs are attracted to a pile of freely available baits.

Make your collection of fruits and vegetables, choosing those that are as ripe as possible. Cut them open so that the flesh is exposed. If you have a greengrocer's plastic-mesh onion bag, or some orange nets from the supermarket, put the baits inside, tie up securely and then put them outside somewhere. Choose open and exposed sites, or protected, sheltered ones. Wherever you put

Pegs

Netting

Are exotic baits like sweet potatoes, peppers, pineapples or chillies eaten?

Were invertebrates seen on citrus fruits like orange, satsuma or lemon?

34

them, hold the bags down with tent pegs. Alternatively, lay some garden netting over the bait and peg it to the ground.

Nibbling mice and voles might be tempted by what you put out, but the immovable mesh bag makes the act of theft much more difficult for them.

You can also hollow out larger and heavier fruits and vegetables, like that old Halloween pumpkin or a giant slice of watermelon, leaving plenty for creatures to eat. Half-bury them so that the flesh can be eaten from above ground and also from below ground by creatures seldom seen at the surface. Leave some fruits and vegetables under discarded plant pots, among logs or in long grass and loosely covered with old sacking.

Thick slices of cucumber will attract snails, if you're looking for them especially.

See The Zoo Zone (pages 42-53).

Inspect the pile of food during the day and at night. Which animals are nocturnal and which are diurnal?

Which minibeasts ate tough-skinned fruits and vegetables?

Old bones (not for wimps)

Luckily there are a few, very useful invertebrates partial to dead meat. Without them wild places would be littered with the stinking carcasses of dead vertebrates. Indeed, forensic scientists depend on using invertebrates to help them to discover when human murder victims were killed. Each minibeast species visiting a corpse does so in a special order. You too can be a forensic investigator and work out which are the first and last to visit the trap below.

Wear a pair of thin rubber gloves for this.

Next time the cat brings in a fresh bird or mouse corpse, leave it in the open and watch how it disappears. Alternatively, a pork chop, meaty bones from a butcher or some chicken wings will also attract a variety of rarely-seen invertebrates. Do your studies well away from the house during warm summer weather because decomposing meat can create some nasty niffs, easily detected by marvellous sexton beetles.

Choose a bare site where you can scratch at the surface to make the soil loose and crumbly.

Tie one end of the nylon fishing line to the bait and the other end to a long nail. Push the nail deep into the ground.

Put the corpse/meat on top of the soil. Cover it with large-mesh garden netting secured with plenty of tent pegs so that hedgehogs and foxes won't be able to carry the bait away. Leave the meat out for about a week.

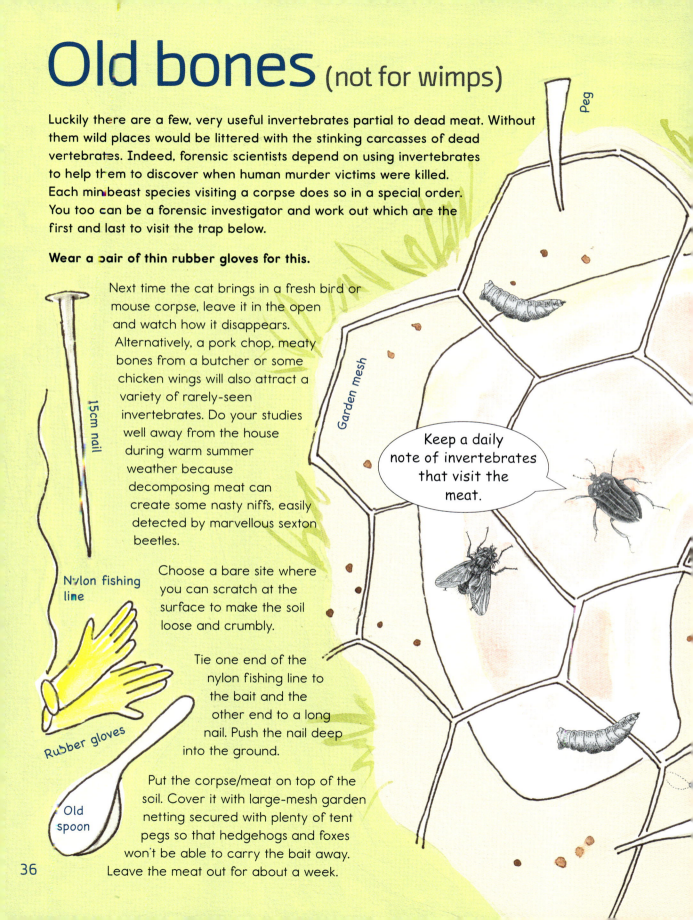

15cm nail

Nylon fishing line

Rubber gloves

Old spoon

Peg

Garden mesh

Keep a daily note of invertebrates that visit the meat.

If a pair of burying or sexton beetles shows interest in the meat, you'll notice it slowly disappearing as they sink it into the graveyard of the soil. This is where the male will guard the corpse and the female will lay her eggs and tend the young. If you want to see the private side of beetle family life, carefully follow the fishing line down to the underground 'crypt', gently scraping away the soil with an old spoon. Wear the gloves for this. You may find the female beetle and her developing larvae within and under the meat. The larvae develop really quickly and are full grown in seven days, so timing is crucial.

Moth punch

For a couple of hundred years lepidopterists have used sugar lures to attract some species of moths. Their recipes were closely guarded secrets, but the basic ingredients were and still are sweeteners (sugar and overripe bananas), an aromatic attractant (pear drops or something yeasty) and some alcohol. The alcohol is to make the moths drowsy so they don't fly away before you've had time to identify them. Moth punch works best on still, moonless, mild and humid nights and away from heavily-scented blossoms.

The recipe to try, but ask an adult to help.

To a large saucepan add flat beer and some dark muscovado sugar or black treacle and simmer for about 10 minutes. If you can get hold of some traditional pear drop sweets, drop them in while the mixture is still hot. Let it cool and then add some rum or stale wine. Add mashed banana, orange or apple juice. Some lepidopterists swear by adding very mature watermelon. The mixture should be so thick that it doesn't drip – a bit like gloopy paint. Soak lengths of clean rope, thick curtain cord or plaited towel strips in the bait. Leave it at room temperature for a day or so to ferment.

About an hour before dusk, fix the baited rope to a tree, fence, or even pegged to a washing line. Throughout the evening check on your visitors by using a torch with red plastic film over the end. The moths can't see red easily, so they won't be disturbed while you look at them. Try painting the mix on grasses, broad-leaved plants and tree trunks.

Light traps

100W incandescent bulb

LED camping lamp

Wide mouthed jar

Some night-flying insects have a fascination for light. They fly crazily round street lamps, porch lights and other light sources, so make the most of this habit to encourage them to come to you.

On dark and moonless nights when the air is warm and humid, open an upstairs window and leave a bright 100W incandescent light bulb running. This may mean temporarily swapping your usual energy-saving bulb. Warn the neighbours of course, and ask an adult to change light bulbs. Watch and wait as the moths fly in. You will have spectacular results if you live out in the wilds where competing bright lights are scarce.

Once a moth has settled on a surface, quickly put a wide-mouthed container over it, slide a postcard under it and then pop on a lid. Now you can study your captive or photograph it. Keep your captive cool and away from bright light. A moth's wings damage very easily when they flap about in a temporary prison, so release the moth on the following evening after the birds have stopped hunting.

You can use the same principle when you peg an old white sheet on a hedge or fence. Stand a LED battery-operated camping lamp on a raised and stable object in front of the sheet.

Both these methods work best if street lamps are some distance away and you can leave lights burning for several hours. Make sure you've got plenty of charged batteries to hand.

The very best way to attract large numbers of moths is with a Mercury Vapour (MV) lamp, so look out for moth-trapping events in your area run by local enthusiasts. You will learn how to identify the larger moths and gather lots of extra interesting facts at the same time.

The Zoo Zone

As you've already discovered, the magic in studying invertebrates is in getting down to their level and catching them unawares with all sorts of ingenious traps. Their lifestyles are totally absorbing and worthy of much closer study.

If you have ever wondered how to keep very small animals as temporary guests, the Zoo Zone is for you. Nothing more complicated than some plastic sweet jars, lemonade bottles, an old clear fish tank and a plant propagator are required.

Snails may be sleepy, but they'll surprise you. Watch them make the next generation of snails. It's a labour of extreme patience, and not just for the snails!

Bottled worms reveal the secrets of their underground world. How can you find out what worms are eating?

Sluggish snails

Garden snails make excellent pets. Adults have robust chunky shells which makes them easy to pick up and handle without you becoming 'slimed'. They can be kept for a few months if you keep them moist and feed them regularly; baby snails, if they are produced, are fascinating to watch.

Setting up home

- If you've got a spare, clear plastic fish tank with a lid, turn it into a snail paradise, arranged as shown. Add some cuttlefish bone bought in a pet shop. It's a rich source of calcium, the very stuff snails need to help them grow strong shells and make their 'love darts'.
- Plant a few common weeds in the soil and add some leaf litter. Spray everything with a water mister.
- Give the snails somewhere to hide during the day – broken clay flowerpots or old tiles make good shelters.
- There's no need for a water dish. Snails get all the moisture they need from food and the water mister.

Finding snails

Look for snails in your **Nooks and Crannies** arrangement and if they are gummed into their shells, you can rouse them gently by putting them in a dish of very shallow warm water. Leave them for about ten minutes, but keep a close eye on them. Once garden snails are awake and active they move fast, so stay alert. Easier still, is to search for them 'running around' on walls and rockeries on warm, damp evenings. Once you've found some, put the snails in their new home

Things to look out for

- Snail poo has a fun element! Try feeding snails on sliced beetroot for a couple of days, then on white kitchen towel. Follow with lettuce for a time, then carrot and so on. Watch out for the rainbow effect. Avoid giving snails cabbage; it makes their poo smelly.

- As the snails glide along the clear sides of their warm, moist tank, you will see on their muscular foot dark and slightly paler alternating bands of muscle movement. Snails can only go forwards, there's no reverse gear.
- Mating. Male and female parts are within the same animal (they are hermaphrodites) – a very good idea if finding each other doesn't depend on speed. Early morning is a good time to see the evidence of snails having mated. They may be side by side with a thick, white tube passing between them. They may also have a thin, white calcareous 'love dart' looking like a single spine poking out of their bodies. Sometimes the darts are left behind on the soil, although the snails often eat them later. After a week or more, both snails will make a depression in the soil where up to 80 or so pearly-white eggs will be laid.
- Young. When the young snails hatch, they will stay in a mass, but eventually venture away from each other. You'll soon see the shell patterns emerging, and just watch those youngsters go! They're much faster than their parents.

Snails on holiday

Snails are one of the few pets that can safely be left alone for a couple of weeks. They're the super-survivors of the mollusc world. They hibernate in winter by sealing themselves in their shells with thick mucus, which dries up over the shell's mouth. In long, dry summers, they do exactly the same. The snail remains moist in its perfectly-sized capsule. Before you go away, remove any stale uneaten food and let the soil dry out. The snails will sense this and gum themselves into their shells. A warm shallow water bath will wake them on your return.

Regularly spray inside the tank with a water mister. Scuff up the soil from time to time, keeping a look out for any mould.

Porridge oats on a jam jar lid.

Scuttle for a spider

Plastic sweet jar

Couple of twigs for support

Sponge

Cotton wool

Mesh

Rubber band

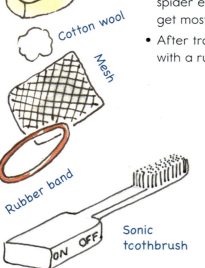

Sonic toothbrush

Spider watching can be enormously engrossing, whether you choose a garden spider or a house spider. Garden spiders need plenty of space for constructing their webs, so to keep one would require a very large tank. The very best way to have a special one is to find an individual that has already built a web outside. Put a painted cane next to the web you want to watch and keep a record of what the spider catches and how often it feeds.

However, everyone's home has a large house spider somewhere, either indoors or out in the garden. They're much the easiest spiders to look after – once you've caught one!

Setting up home

- Ask an adult to make a 1cm wide hole on the top side of the jar.
- Put a plug of cotton wool or, even better, sponge in the hole to prevent the spider escaping – this is the entry point for prey and a little water. Spiders get most of their liquid from food, so be mean with water.
- After transferring your spider to the sweet jar, firmly attach a fine-mesh top with a rubber band.

Finding spiders

There are two cunning ways of trapping a spider.

1) Look out for one rushing across the carpet in autumn, when male spiders are busy searching for a female. Wait until he stops running. Put a wide-mouthed jar over him and slide a piece of card between the jar and the floor. Once you've trapped the spider, turn the jar upside down, so you can pop a lid on. Transfer him to his living accommodation. Spiders rarely live together, so don't feel sorry for him as you give him a home to himself.

2) This is a truly amazing way of enticing a spider to run out onto its web. You will need skill and another person to help you. Look for a large white, often triangular sheet web. Ivy-covered fences and walls are good places to start, as are sheds and secluded corners of gardens. The web leads down to a narrow tube retreat where the spider will be lurking. Have the sonic toothbrush switched on and trembling.

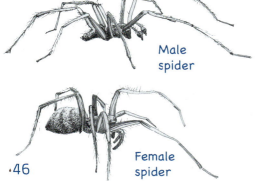

Male spider

Female spider

READ THE NEXT BIT CAREFULLY. Ask a friend to lightly touch the underneath of the web. The spider should come charging out at high speed to sit on top of the web. Here's where you need to act fast; you'll need both hands. While the spider's on its web and still confused, place a wide mouthed jar over it and a lid under it. The spider is now trapped on its own web. Lift the jar, spider and lid clear of the web. Transfer the spider to its new home and wait for a new web to appear.

Things to look out for

- Confirming males and females. Spiders have eight legs, but look closely. Are you counting ten of them? The very short 'legs' at the head end near the fangs are actually palps. On mature males the ends of the palps are swollen, like boxing gloves, and are used for transferring sperm. Female palps have no swellings.
- When the spider has produced a new web, pop in the first fly. Don't spend too long blinking.
- A female spider might make a creamy-white egg sac. She may stick fragments of prey items onto the sac as camouflage – disgusting to predators but nursery decoration to 'mum'. Wait a few weeks and the spider-lings will hatch. They're gorgeous – powder blue! Release them quickly. They're not brotherly or sisterly.
- A young spider will cast off its almost transparent 'skin' leaving it on the web. Look at the 'skin' with a strong lens or even better, a microscope.
- Spiders are good housekeepers. They usually pile their rubbish in one place.
- Spiders are remarkably keen on cleaning themselves. They spend many minutes passing each leg in turn through their mouthparts.

47

Entertaining earwigs

Earwigs are not the villains most people believe them to be, and are engaging insects to watch. They are largely nocturnal, but if you follow the plan on this page, you will be tricking the earwigs into believing that the nights are very long, and that daylight appears in brief flashes; all the better for your observations. Earwigs are easily lured to a flower-pot trap stuffed with straw or screwed-up newspaper (see **Nooks and Crannies**, page 18). They eat huge numbers of aphids and other plant pests, so encourage the gardeners in your house to indulge them. Female earwigs are truly amazing mothers, only leaving their youngsters when they are almost mature.

Setting up home

- Ask an adult to microwave some damp sand or soil for 10 minutes. This is to prevent mould from growing. Wait for it to go completely cold. Put the sand or soil in the bottom of a sweet jar.
- Have some short lengths (15-20cm) of clear polythene tubing ready, held together with a rubber band. The tubing should have a diameter similar to that of a wide drinking straw. You could make your own earwig tubes by loosely rolling some stiff transparent plastic document sleeves. Stand the bunch of tubes upright.

Male earwig Female earwig

Clear drinking straws or polythene tubing

Chopped dried or fresh fruit.
Cucumber.
A little cat or dog food

Foil dish

Microwaved damp sand or soil

48

Black paper

- Measure and cut enough black paper or plastic to wrap loosely round the sweet jar and seal the two edges with strong tape. You need to be able to slide the black covering up and down to spy on the creatures inside.
- Get a small piece of foil to use as a food dish.

Finding earwigs

After the earwig trap has been in place for a few weeks, tip everything into a shallow tray. Either poot the earwigs, or pick them up with tweezers. Another way to find earwigs is to look for dried, hollow plant stems in autumn. Give several stems a good thwack against the inside of an empty sweet jar and animals will come tumbling out. Sort out the number of earwigs you want (see below) and move them into their new home.

Things to look out for

- Telling males from females. Male earwigs have large and curved rear pincers, while those of the female are shorter and straight. Annoyed males curl their rear ends forward in an attack movement, so keep clear of earwig bottoms! A nip from one won't hurt, but you'll be amazed at how long such a small creature can hang on for. Count the number of male and female earwigs you've caught and try to have equal numbers of each, although males won't mind being outnumbered by females. Four to six earwigs should be sufficient for your observations. Don't forget to put tightly fitting fine mesh over the open top.
- You'll be able to see your new pets resting in their transparent tubes or feeding when you slide the cover up. Spray the soil in the jar from time to time, but don't overdo it.
- In autumn earwigs mate. Not many people have seen this – you could be one of the lucky ones. Stand the earwig jar in a dark room for a day or two because you need double-dark for this. Slowly and quietly slide away the black cover, because earwigs are very sensitive to sound and movement. They can't see red light, so a lamp with a red bulb or a LED torch with a red filter might allow you a brief glimpse of something very special indeed.
- Already-mated female earwigs caught in early spring, might lay batches of ivory-coloured eggs in the soil or under small flat stones. These eggs are guarded with their mothers' lives. The eggs are turned and licked to prevent mould from attacking. When the young hatch, they look like minute adults, because they don't have a larval stage like most other insects. 'Mum' will dote on her little white 'wiglets' for weeks, feeding and tending them. When your investigations are over let them all go together, gently tipping them out so that the mother can gather all her babies in one place.

Red torch or rear bike lamp

49

Wonderful wallowing worms

Why are worms wonderful? Of all the invertebrates on the planet, worms are the multiple award-winners – what would plants and all the rest of life do without them? They plough and burrow through the soil, fertilising it and keeping it in tip-top condition as they go. Wallowing in mud is what they do best and here's a way of spying on their activities.

Setting up home

You can make a very simple wormery using two lemonade bottles.

- Put sand in the bottom of the 2 litre bottle.
- Invert the closed 250ml bottle and push it into the sand in the 2 litre bottle.
- Fill the gap between the two bottles with alternate layers of dark and light soil.
- Bang the bottle hard to settle the soil. Add 4-6 worms. Feed with porridge oats and chopped-up wet leaf litter.
- Secure fine netting on the top with a rubber band. Wrap with black paper/plastic and wait for a week.
- Be kind to the worm farm by keeping it cool.
- Remove the black covering to watch the action.

Wash worms with clean rain water.

Finding worms

You can dig for worms in the vegetable garden on dusky evenings after rain, or use the following 'worm charming' method. Look for worm casts in the short grass of a lawn. They resemble coils of thin brown toothpaste that has been squirted up from beneath your feet. Worms also pull leaves and other detritus into their burrows, leaving stalks or leaf tips poking out. Mark a circle on the grass round the worm signs with a length of string, or use a hula hoop. Water the grass inside the hoop really well allowing it to soak in. You might have to do this a few times especially in dry weather. Now get your friends to perform a crazy jumping or zumba competition round the circle until the first worms 'peep' out, except of course worms don't have proper eyes. Sprinkle emerging worms with water containing very, very dilute washing-up liquid and they should come to the surface at speed.

Wash them quickly and thoroughly in plain rainwater to remove itchy traces of detergent.

Important: Never pull a worm out of its burrow. You will damage it.

Things to look out for
- Check your wormery for burrows and signs of oat flakes or leaves being pulled into the soil.
- After a while, are the coloured soil layers beginning to mix?
- Look to see whether at night, the worms come to the surface to mate. They lie next to each other with their thickened 'waist' bands touching.

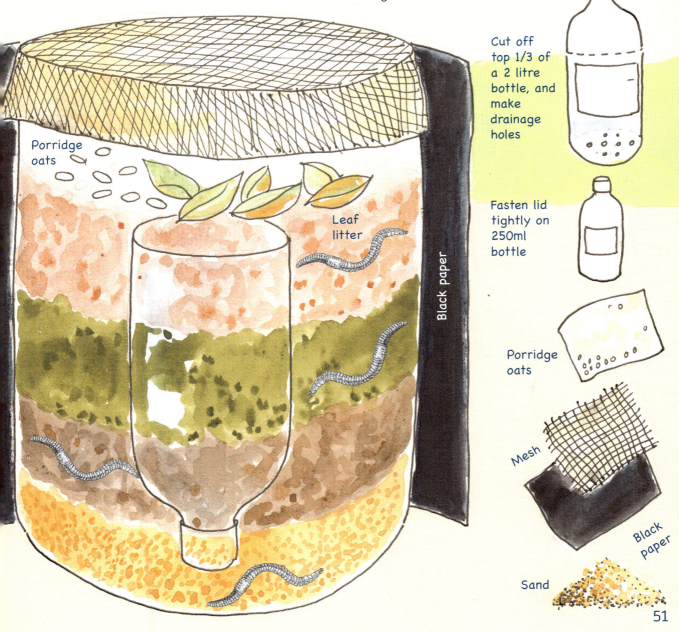

Nature reserve
for invertebrates

Here's how to have some of the outside, IN-side! Set up this nature reserve, or mini-zoo, in a plastic (unheated) plant propagator.

Setting up home

- Clean the propagator and rinse it thoroughly.
- Open the top vents and cover them over with fine netting fixed with double-sided sticky tape.
- Half fill the bottom tray of the propagator with good garden soil. Add a piece of gently rotting wood and other 'furniture' for creatures to hide in and graze on, for example an old, broken clay pot with a covering of green algae. Even an old tennis ball sliced open makes a good hiding place, as do empty snail shells and pine cones.
- Plant some common garden weeds in the gaps.
- Cuttlefish bone is a kind addition for any snails.
- Top everything off with a good layer of damp leaf litter and leave the propagator in a cool but well-lit place to let the growing plants settle for a week or two. Then move to a shady place, well away from sunlight.

WARNING Exclude ants in the reserve - they will escape.

Woodlice and millipedes eat rotting wood and softening leaves. Up to 10 woodlice and 3 or 4 millipedes will live happily together.

Top off with good layer of damp leaf litter

Worms will feed on leaf litter. Add two or three.

Other inhabitants can include a small snail or two and a slug. Big ones that look as though they're wearing ribbed jumpers make a mess.

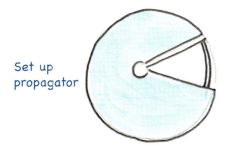

Set up propagator

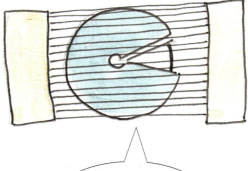

Leave to settle for a week or two

Keep vents open. Cover with fine mesh.

Finding inmates

Easy – collect animals from any of the previous traps.

Reserve Manager's Responsibilities

1. Keep a close eye on your zoo animals.

2. Give them some treats. Add a few potato peelings or cucumber slices for the herbivores and detritivores and smears of meaty pet food for the carnivores.

3. Some animals might breed. Remove the carnivores if you want to watch young snails grow up or count baby woodlice.

4. Look out for woodlouse moult skins. They moult in two halves, back end first, and then the front.

5. It won't rain in the reserve. Condensation will run down the sides of the lid and trickle into the edges of the soil, but a desert in the centre could develop, so spray it occasionally.

6. There will be mystery visitors to your reserve too. The ones that arrived on the bit of log, caterpillars on weed leaves, pupae and larvae in the soil, minute jumping springtails, earwigs and more, so keep watch.

7. And finally, when you decide to let your animals explore the wider world outside, release them on a mild evening.

Fast runners like spiders and harvestmen might escape when you lift the lid.

Ground beetles and the chestnut-coloured centipedes are top predators, so only choose one of each.

Finally... other favourites

There are lots of other animals you can rear for fun, such as:

Caterpillars

Keep a look out for caterpillars, noticing what leaves they are feeding on. Cut the food plant so that it has stems and plenty of leaves. Put a small pot filled with wet sand in the bottom of a sweet jar or large water carrier and put the cut stems in the sand. Change the leaves faster than the caterpillars can eat them. The caterpillars won't escape if you secure some fine mesh over the top. They will each make a pupa. Some prefer to bury themselves at this stage, so put microwaved soil in the sweet jar base. Others stick themselves to the plant. How long will you have to wait for the moth or butterfly? If what emerges is neither of those, what could it be? Identification book at the ready!

Ladybirds

Ladybirds appear every spring and so do their favourite food – greenflies or aphids. Find a good source of greenflies clustering at the growing tips of plants. Each day brush them into a small pot and tip them into the keeping container. Don't miss a single day, because ladybirds are voracious predators. Keep them as you would caterpillars with fresh stems in the wet sand. Look for yellow ladybird eggs laid on the underside of leaves and put them outside near a plant covered in greenfly. The little black larvae are quite difficult to rear unless you've got aphids of the right size, but you can learn a lot by having a try.

Woodlice

Put some garden soil in the bottom of a deep ice-cream tub and add all sorts of quietly rotting wood. Collect up woodlice of all sizes. Look under stones and plant pots to find them. Once added, fix fine mesh over the open top. The larger ones will be mature and may mate and produce young. Female woodlice give 'birth' to live babies, releasing them from flaps on their undersides. The babies look just like 'mum' and 'dad' and are white at first, but tiny. They're called mancas. Do woodlice have any other food preferences?

Who's who

A who's who directory to creatures on the trap pages.

These illustrations are just a guide to the animals you may find in your traps. Most invertebrate groups contain many species, so for accurate identifications go to some of the field guides mentioned in the further reading list. If you have a thirst for the biological Latin names of the creatures, you will learn those too. There are some fabulous-sounding names to get your tongue around!

Approximate sizes are shown in millimetres (mm) and indicate length of body from head to tail. Antennae are not included.

Woodlice

Pill woodlouse (10mm)   Common woodlouse (10mm)

Worms

Common earthworm (up to 300mm)

Millipedes

Snake millipede (up to 50mm)

Pill millipede (up to 20mm long and 8mm wide)

Flat-backed millipede (up to 25mm long and 4mm wide)

Slugs

Large ribbed slug (up to 100mm)

Snails

Garden snail (up to 35mm)

Door snail (15mm)   Flat snail (7mm)

Centipedes

Chestnut centipede (up to 30mm)

Yellow centipede (up to 45mm)

Continued over...

Who's who (continued)

Insects

Springtail (3mm)

Aphid (2mm)

Solitary bee (13mm)

Shield bug (up to 15mm)

Leaf hopper (8mm)

Mirid bug (6-8mm)

Ant (4-6mm)

Lacewing (20mm)

Earwig (20mm)

2-spot ladybird (5mm)

Scorpion fly (15mm)

Fruit fly (4mm)

Grasshopper (up to 27mm)

Bluebottle fly (9mm)

Crane fly (25mm)

Ground beetle (20-30mm)

Devil's coach-horse beetle (20-30mm)

Sap beetle (3-7mm)

Rove beetle (7-9mm)

Common wasp (18mm)

Bumblebee (20mm)

Chafer beetle (7-12mm)

Burying beetle (19mm)

Red-breasted carrion beetle (11-16mm)

Arachnids

False scorpion (up to 4mm)

Velvet mite (up to 3mm)

Weevil (up to 11mm)

Bluebottle larva (10mm)

Ladybird larva (up to 7mm)

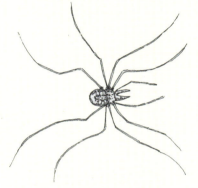

Harvestman (up to 9mm)

Caterpillars (from 5-60mm)

Garden spider (up to 18mm)

Hunting spider (up to 9mm)

Elephant hawk moth (50-60mm wingspan)

Large house spider (up to 16mm)

Meadow brown butterfly (40-50mm wingspan)

Further reading

Nick Baker, *Nick Baker's Bug Book: Discover the World of the Minibeast* (New Holland Publishers Ltd 2011).
An inspirational book that expands on many of the topics in *Minibeast Magic*.

Peter Smithers & John Walters, *Minibeasts – An Identification Guide* (John Walters 2004).
A companion guide to *Minibeast Magic* with keys to major groups of invertebrates, colour illustrations and photographs. Currently being revised.

Other useful publications

Insects (mostly)

Michael Chinery, *Insects of Britain & Western Europe* (Collins Field Guide 2012).
This is the bible for insect spotters everywhere, with over 2,000 colour illustrations for identification of adult insects and some larvae. Valuable end pages cover other arthropods such as centipedes, millipedes, woodlice, spiders and other arachnids.

Michael Chinery, *Complete Guide to British Insects* (Collins 2009).
A photographic guide to British insects covering 1,500 species.

Michael Chinery, *Insects of Britain and Northern Europe* (Collins Field Guide 1993).
A thoroughly comprehensive guide to the lives of insects. Contains keys to all major groups of insects.

Michael Chinery & Bob Gibbons, *Collins Gem Book of Insects* (2012).
Small, portable and covers 240 insects. Good introduction to the various groups.

Bob Gibbons, *Field Guide to the Insects of Britain and Northern Europe* (The Crowood Press 1996).
Brilliant photographs of most common insects.

George C. McGavin, *Insects. A Dorling Kindersley Handbook* (2010).
Includes spiders and terrestrial arthropods. Detailed background information and descriptions. Some species non-British. Wonderful photographs.

George C. McGavin, *Insects and Spiders.* (Dorling Kindersley Pocket Nature Guide 2005).
A photographic guide, and an identification and reference book.

Anthony Wooton, *Bugs. Usborne Spotter's Guide* (2006).

Pamela Forey & Cecelia Fitzsimons, *Identification Guide – Insects* (Flame Tree Publishing 2007).

Garden wildlife

Michael Chinery, *Garden Creepy-Crawlies* (Whittet Books 1986).
Interesting and amusing book on garden invertebrates, with highly readable information. Will be difficult to put down. Not an identification book. Unfortunately out of print.

Michael Chinery, *Garden Wildlife of Britain and Europe* (Collins Nature Guide 1997).
Includes plants and vertebrates.

Richard Lewington, *Guide to Garden Wildlife* (British Wildlife Publishing 2008).
Includes vertebrates.

Butterflies & moths

Paul Waring & Martin Townsend, *Concise Guide to the Moths of Great Britain and Ireland* (British Wildlife Publishing 2007).
Possibly the best book for moths with stunning illustrations by Richard Lewington.

Richard Lewington, *Pocket Guide to the Butterflies of Great Britain and Ireland* (British Wildlife Publishing 2003).
Again, wonderful information and illustrations by the author.

George C. McGavin, *Butterflies.* A Pocket Spotter Guide (2003).

George E. Hyde, *Butterflies.* Usborne Spotter's Guide (2006).

UK moths website – visit
http://ukmoths.org.uk/top20.php
This is a great website – you should be able to identify the vast majority of your larger moths here.

All invertebrates and general insects

Field Studies Council charts – visit http://www.field-studies-council.org/publications/fold-out-charts.aspx
These are excellent guides to a whole range of invertebrates such as butterfly caterpillars, house and garden spiders, and ladybirds.

http://www.royensoc.co.uk/insect_info/what_is_it.htm
Visit this Royal Entomological Society website for fascinating facts and guides to the major insect groups.

Mark Fellowes & Amanda Callaghan, *Garden Entomology* (Royal Entomological Society)
Available free of charge from the Royal Entomological Society, this guide picks out some of the insects that you are likely to see in gardens around the UK.

And finally, for a bit of factual fun

Anneliese Emmans Dean, *Buzzing* (Brambleby Books 2012).
A fascinating mix of amusing poems, wonderful photographs and intriguing minibeast facts.

www.amentsoc.org/bug-club/
The Bug Club is for youngsters age 13 and under. Their magazine is packed with articles on all sorts of British invertebrates. There are six issues a year.

Glossary

Are there some unusual words that you've not come across before? Find out what they mean here.

Adaptations – features or habits that make an invertebrate fit for its habitat or environment, e.g. a thin, muscular worm is adapted to move through soil.

Arthropods – animals with rigid external skeletons and jointed legs.

Biological – everything to do with living organisms (animals and plants).

Calcareous – made of calcium.

Carnivores – invertebrates that consume living animals.

Carrion – decomposing animal matter.

Cephalothorax – the head and 'chest' region on a spider.

Corpse – a dead body.

Detritivores – invertebrates that consume dead and decaying organisms.

Detritus – dead and accumulated matter from once living organisms.

Diurnal – animals active during daylight hours.

Entomologist – a scientist who is an insect specialist.

Entomology – the science of insects.

Exoskeleton – the rigid outside parts of arthropods.

Fissures – very narrow openings, like a groove.

Fauna – a group of animals.

Habitat – the usual living space for an animal or plant.

Herbivores – invertebrates that consume living plants.

Invertebrate – a small animal with no backbone or internal skeleton.

Larva – an immature stage of an insect that looks completely different to the adult.

Lepidopterist – someone who studies moths and butterflies.

Nocturnal – an animal that is active at night.

Nymph – an immature stage of an insect that looks like a miniature adult.

Organism – any living plant or animal.

Palps – the sensory organs on the heads of spiders.

Pupa – the 'resting' or changing phase of a fully grown insect larva. It does not feed or move.

Species – groups of animals or plants that share common features. They cannot interbreed with other groups.

Vertebrate – an animal with a backbone.